# Philosophers

PEOPLE YOU NEED TO KNOW

SUSANNA WRIGHT

WAYLAND

www.waylandbooks.co.u

First published in Great Britain in 2019
by Wayland
Copyright © Hodder and Stoughton, 2019
Illustrations copyright © 2019
by Susanna Wright

Wayland, an imprint of
Hachette Children's Group
Part of Hodder and Stoughton
Carmelite House
50 Victoria Embankment
London EC4Y 0DZ

An Hachette UK Company
www.hachette.co.uk
www.hachettechildrens.co.uk

ISBN 978 1 5263 0532 9

FSC
www.fsc.org
MIX
Paper from
responsible sources
FSC® C104740

Printed and bound in China

Design by Cathryn Gilbert and Peter Scoulding
Edited by Paul Rockett

# Contents

# Philosophy

The word PHILOSOPHY comes from ancient Greek roots: *philo* meaning love and *sophos* meaning wisdom – so philosophy is the love of wisdom. Wisdom, in this case, means the ability to reason: to question what we think, what we believe and what we hold to be true, and to ask why. Philosophers ask big questions, such as: can we ever really know anything? Do we have free will? What happens after death? Does life have meaning? How can we achieve happiness? How can we build a better, fairer society – and why should we?

The Philosophical Method is a long-established technique that philosophers have used to try to find answers to these questions. This method involves doubting our own accepted beliefs (so not just following popular thinking), making our question as clear and precise as possible, coming up with a theory that attempts to answer the question, and then using logic to construct 'arguments': a set of clear statements to support our theory. At this point, others must test the argument and try to find the weaknesses in the theory. Through this process, philosophers try to tackle big questions and discover fundamental truths.

There are lots of different branches of philosophy, and the history of philosophy has roots all over the world. The people depicted in this book are just a few interesting figures in a rich, complex and ever-extending discipline.

Philosophy was the beginning of many of the most important subjects of study that we use to investigate our world – what we now think of as science was originally a part of philosophy, as were astronomy, physics, medicine, sociology, psychology, economics and linguistics. Philosophy has led us to study the cosmos, our planet, our minds, our emotions, our beliefs, our systems for living, our conception of what is good or bad, and to wonder if any of what we have perceived during these investigations is 'real', and what 'real' might mean. It is an adventure into the very heart of what it means to exist.

# GARGI VACHAKNAVI

## 7TH CENTURY BCE

 I rise to fell you with two questions.

GARGI VACHAKNAVI was an Indian philosopher who challenged the conventional thinking of her time. She possessed great knowledge of the *Vedas*: ancient Indian texts which reflect the oldest teachings of Hinduism.

In the kingdom of Videhar (a province between eastern India and Nepal), King Janaka filled his court with the notable minds of his era – he called them his 'nine gems'. One of these was Gargi, who wrote many of the hymns in the *Rig Veda*, one of the four sacred texts of Hinduism. It was here that she attended the world's first philosophy conference, where a man who was considered the wisest in the world – Yajnavalkya – was questioned at the King's order.

Gargi asked, "That which is above heaven and below the earth, which is the same through past, present and future – in what is that woven?" Yajnavalkya answered, "In space." Gargi then asked, "In what is space itself woven." He answered, "The imperishable." When she asked what the world of the Imperishable was made of she was told not to question beyond that, "lest your head fall off." Gargi was examining the nature of time and space; her thinking threatened to destabilise religious teachings on the source of existence.

She was a true philosopher, seeking truths beyond accepted beliefs.

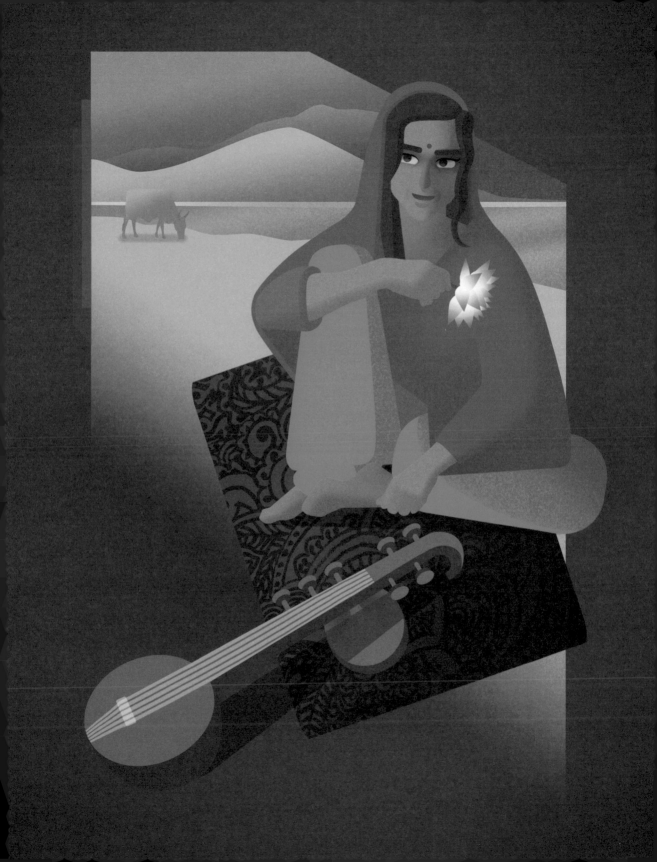

# CONFUCIUS

551 – 479 BCE

" *Our greatest glory is not in never falling, but in rising every time we fall.* "

CONFUCIUS was a philosopher, teacher and statesman who is arguably the most influential person in Chinese history. He strongly believed that self-improvement through education should be available to all as the basis for social order and peace.

Confucius lived during a time of great change known as the Spring and Autumn Period, when long-held traditions and political relations were shaken. This resulted in what he saw as a decline in moral standards, and so he considered it his responsibility to teach the value of compassion and tradition. The core of his philosophy was based around the principle of ren: treating others with humanity and kindness. He believed that ren could be manifested via his Golden Rule: what you do not wish for yourself, do not do to others.

In education, Confucius focused on the Six Arts – ritual, mathematics, archery, music, calligraphy and chariot-driving – but his central theme was to teach people to behave with integrity. This was also reflected in his political beliefs, which led him to urge leaders to remain humble and compassionate.

Confucius wrote many works, including *Lunyu* (translated into English as *The Analects of Confucius*) which, by outlining his political and philosophical values, helped to secure him a deep and lasting influence. The ethical teachings which he did not see implemented in his lifetime have, for the last two thousand years, been core to morality, education, law and politics in China.

# SOCRATES

c.470 – 399 BCE

 The unexamined life is not worth living.

SOCRATES was a Greek philosopher whose teachings had a profound influence on the Western world. Based in Athens, he engaged his students in conversations where he asked questions that encouraged them to find their own logical conclusions. This approach was called the Socratic Method.

It is only through the writings of others – most famously the philosopher Plato (who was his student) in his *Platonic Dialogues* – that we know about Socrates at all.

Socrates believed that philosophy ought to improve society in practical ways: it should lead to an ethical system which was not undermined by religion or tradition. He thought that government shouldn't be a democracy or a tyranny, but be run by the most virtuous and knowledgeable people among us. Plato captured Socrates' vision of this 'ideal state' in his work *The Republic*.

Socrates believed that the more a person knows the more able they will be to reason and make choices – and therefore they will be happier. This caused him to say, "There is only one good, knowledge, and one evil, ignorance."

His teachings were threatening to some: he likened himself to a 'gadfly' bothering the state, reminding it of its duties. This irreverence led to him being found guilty of impiety (lack of respect for religion) at the age of 70, and he was ordered to drink poison made from hemlock. Although he had an opportunity to escape, Socrates chose not to flee, and used his execution as a final lesson for his pupils: facing death calmly, surrounded by friends.

# PLATO

## c.427 – 347 BCE

> " Thinking: the talking of the soul with itself. "

PLATO is one of the most dazzling and influential figures in the history of Western philosophy. Born in Athens, Plato was a student of Socrates, whose influence can be found in most of Plato's thirty-six books (or 'dialogues'). Plato also founded the first institution of higher learning: The Academy in Athens.

One of his ideas was the Theory of Forms, found in his book *Timaeus* (c.360 BCE). In this dialogue he attempts to explain the order he sees in the Universe, partially inspired by Platonic solids (five 3D shapes that have a perfectly symmetrical arrangement of points in space). He thought of a Form as an eternal ideal, like a spiritual blueprint – and all things in existence were imperfect versions of these ideals. Plato believed there were two realms: the world of the senses which we live in, and the non-physical realm of the Forms.

This idea is also reflected in the 'Allegory of the Cave', one of the stories in *The Republic* (c.380 BCE). In it he describes people in a cave watching shadows being cast by a puppet show they can't see; they believe the shadows to be 'reality' but are unaware of their true source. This story communicates Plato's belief that only through reasoning can a person free themselves of their mistaken beliefs – in other words escape 'the cave' – and get closer to the Forms.

All things for Plato have a Form – love, friendship, government, as well as objects and lifeforms. Through philosophical thought a person could reason their way closer to these ideal states and therefore build a more fulfilled life.

# ARISTOTLE

384 – 322 BCE

"
In all things of nature there is something of the marvellous.
"

Known as 'The Master', ARISTOTLE was an influential intellectual powerhouse who transformed the areas of knowledge he immersed himself in. These included metaphysics, mathematics, biology, ethics, politics, agriculture, dance and theatre.

Born in Macedonia in 384, Aristotle went to Athens, where he studied at Plato's Academy. He later set up his own school, known as The Lyceum. He would roam around freely as he taught his students, who came to be known as Peripatetics, meaning 'given to wandering about'.

Aristotle believed that the whole of existence was made up of five elements: earth, water, fire, air and aether (material he thought existed in the space beyond planet Earth). This notion that all matter was made up from these elements held back further exploration into what makes up the world (which we know now to be atoms) for over two thousand years, so well-regarded was every aspect of Aristotle's teachings.

In *Nicomachean Ethics*, Aristotle wrote that we all seek eudaimonia, or "self-flourishings" which can be achieved through developing certain virtues. Offering a list of eleven true virtues, he suggested that each one was the perfect "golden mean" (middle way) between two vices. Happiness was to be found through the rational pursuit of this balancing act, and aiming for virtue was necessary for this quest.

# HYPATIA

c.355 – 415

" Reserve your right to think, for even to think wrongly is better than not to think at all. "

There is some uncertainty about when HYPATIA was born, and whether she was Egyptian or Greek. However, what is certain is that she was exceptional: as well as a philosopher, lecturer and inventor she was a world-leading mathematician and astronomer, and the head of the Neoplatonist School of Philosophy in the city of her birth, Alexandria.

The philosophy Hypatia taught, via hugely popular public lectures, was her interpretation of neoplatonism: a fusion of the teachings of Plato and Aristotle with mystical beliefs. Neoplatonism originated with Plotinus (205 – 270), a Greek-speaking philosopher of the ancient world, who suggested that reality was derived from a single principle: the One. From the One, all the diversity of the Universe flowed – structures and lifeforms that were, as fragments, lesser than the principle from which they came. Hypatia believed that abstract thought and reasoning brought one closer to the One. Her study of the path of the planets and her work with mathematics reflected her commitment to a deeper understanding of what exists, and in her philosophy she encouraged her students to think critically.

In an act of great brutality, Hypatia was murdered by a mob of Christians, who described her writings and inventions as 'witchcraft'. Although she wrote many important works on mathematics and astronomy, none of her books survived the destruction of Alexandria's famed library. Her legacy as a figure of learning and truth-seeking, however, remains.

# RENÉ DESCARTES

## 31 MARCH, 1596 – 11 FEBRUARY, 1650

" I think, therefore I am. "

Born in France, DESCARTES was a scientist and mathematician as well as a philosopher. His ideas led to him being regarded as the 'father of modern philosophy'. He liked thinking in solitude and believed we can answer the most profound questions by searching within ourselves.

In applying logic and mathematics to understanding the natural world, his ideas diverged from the conventions of his time; he attempted to think about the truth in a new way – by looking for what can be determined. Within his work of 1637, *Discourse on the Method*, his famous statement, "I think, therefore I am," reflects the fact that at the very least we can know that we exist, since we have consciousness, and the act of thinking confirms that. He viewed this as a starting point for the further questioning of beliefs, applying a method of doubt now known as Cartesian skepticism (Cartesian meaning relating to Descartes).

Among other achievements, he created the Cartesian coordinate system (giving numerical coordinates to points within a grid) which revolutionised mathematics. His approach to examining the physical world while questioning the metaphysical led him to contemplate mind-body duality – the relationship between the material body and the immaterial mind – considering the pineal gland in the brain to be the point of contact between the body and the soul.

Descartes was a driving force for 17th century rationalism, a movement which suggested that reason rather than experience leads us to certainty in knowledge. He believed that no-one should rely on tradition and that eternal truths could be found through reason alone.

# IMMANUEL KANT

## 22 APRIL, 1724 – 12 FEBRUARY, 1804

> " Science is organised knowledge.
> Wisdom is organised life. "

IMMANUEL KANT was a German philosopher who wrote during the Enlightenment, a period in 18th century Europe when philosophers and thinkers began to focus on reason and logic over religion or tradition.

In 1784, Kant wrote an essay called 'What is Enlightenment?' in which he linked the movement to the decline of Christianity. Kant recognised that religion gave people ethical guidance, so he outlined a desire for an alternative, rational approach to ethics. He wrote that the motto of the Enlightenment was "Have courage to use your own understanding!" His quest for rationally driven ethics led him to develop his most famous concept: the categorical imperative.

The categorical imperative states: "Act only in accordance with that maxim through which you can at the same time will that it become a universal law." Simply put: don't do something unless you would be happy to see everyone do the same; for instance, only steal if you would be happy for it to be legal for anyone to steal from you. Kant felt this was a powerful way to test the morality of a proposed action.

As well as moral philosophy, Kant also wrote about metaphysics – the branch of philosophy which deals with fundamental abstract concepts such as being, reality, time and space. In his book *The Critique of Pure Reason* (1781) he examined the difference between two types of knowledge: that which we gain through experience, and that which we learn independently of experience, such as knowledge found in mathematics and scientific principles.

# MARY WOLLSTONECRAFT

27 APRIL, 1759 – 10 SEPTEMBER, 1797

" Mind has no gender. "

MARY WOLLSTONECRAFT was a philosopher, writer, human rights activist, educational pioneer and translator, and is renowned for being a trailblazing thinker and founder of the feminist movement.

Born in London, Wollstonecraft lived her short life according to her ideals. She established a school for girls in Newington Green in order to further the educational opportunities for women; she also spent two years in France during the French Revolution (because she believed that the reforms should include positive change for women); and engaged in relationships without regard to the societal pressures that restricted women's choices.

Her most famous work is *A Vindication of the Rights of Women* (1792) in which she argued that women were equal to men and equally deserving of education – a controversial idea for the time. Outraged opponents to the idea of gender equality called her "a hyena in petticoats". She argued that both women and men were rational beings, and imagined a new social order founded on fairness and reason.

Her impact on the lives of women to this day is extraordinary: in the 1800s her work inspired the early women's movements in the USA and Europe, which led to the fights for women to have the right to own their own property, keep their own wages, sign a contract on their own, without a man, and have the right to vote. As she wrote, "I do not wish women to have power over men; but over themselves."

# GEORG WILHELM FRIEDRICH HEGEL

27 AUGUST, 1770 – 14 NOVEMBER, 1831

" We learn from history that we
do not learn from history. "

Born in Stuttgart, Germany, GEORG HEGEL was a renowned philosopher of German idealism, a philosophical movement which developed as a reaction to the philosophy of Kant and was linked to Romanticism. In contrast to the rationality of Classicism, Romantics favoured notions of the visionary, the imaginative and the subjective.

In his work, Hegel attempted to create a philosophical system that could allow us to understand the entirety of the past and the future, and other seemingly contradictory ideas at the same time. In his central work *The Phenomenology of Spirit* (1807) he argued that we should consider the development and existence of everything as a complete whole, which he referred to as Absolute Spirit – or *Geist* in German.

He saw historical and social progress as something which wasn't linear: rather it lurched from one extreme to another and, in the process, ideas or qualities from both extremes were integrated, achieving a greater balance. This interplay between oppositions is described as the 'dialectic', although Hegel's phrase was "determinate negation": when two things negate each other (are different, opposing) this interaction causes something new to occur.

Hegel wrote four important books in his lifetime and in them he applied this system of dialectics to the whole of history, philosophy, politics, science, art and religion. His work has had significant impact and influence on many other thinkers. The idea of the dialectic had a profound effect on Karl Marx, who, along with Friedrich Engels, wrote *The Communist Manifesto* in 1848 which led to enormous shifts in the 20th century political landscape.

# SØREN KIERKEGAARD

5 MAY, 1813 – 11 NOVEMBER, 1855

" Life is not a problem to be solved,
but a reality to be experienced. "

Born in Copenhagen, KIERKEGAARD had a crucial influence on subsequent generations of philosophers and was known as the 'father of existentialism' (existentialism being a philosophical approach that believes all philosophical thought begins with the individual, thinking self). It is through his work that the word 'angst' (anxiety or dread) came into common use; his work of 1843, *Fear and Trembling*, was centered around the idea of anxiety. He engaged with the sense of disquiet that comes with existence in a way that predated the psychology of Freud (the renowned psychoanalyst). *Either/Or*, also written in 1843, tackles the contrast between the desire for hedonism (pleasure-seeking) and the desire to be ethical.

Kierkegaard believed that how an individual behaved in response to objective truth was vital. He argued that how one acts is more important than what is fact, and therefore: "subjectivity is truth".

Kierkegaard often used a method of writing called 'indirect communication', where he would write from intellectual positions he disagreed with; he did this in order to provoke the reader into a deeper level of engagement with the ideas involved. It was designed to disrupt the idea that the reader could rely on the authority of the author, therefore encouraging people to take responsibility for their own thinking.

Kierkegaard took refuge in the notion of Christianity, saying that rational thought could not access it: it required a "leap of faith". He hated the Church of the state but loved the notion of an individual path to Christ: he was a deep thinker who found relief in what he described as the "unthink" of religious faith.

# FRIEDRICH NIETZSCHE

### 15 OCTOBER, 1844 – 25 AUGUST, 1900

 *What doesn't kill me makes me stronger.*

NIETZSCHE was a German philosopher, poet and cultural critic whose work had a notable and lasting impact on Western philosophy and modern thought. An unusually brilliant student, Nietzsche was made a professor at the University of Basel in his twenties. He quickly tired of academia and retreated to the Swiss Alps, where he wrote masterpiece after masterpiece, exploring ideas of power and how to escape a meaningless sense of existence (nihilism) through the affirmation of life. Some of his most famous books are *Human, All Too Human*, *Thus Spake Zarathustra* and *Beyond Good And Evil*.

At the age of 44, Nietzsche suffered a mental collapse from which he never recovered (triggered when he witnessed a horse being beaten in the street; he ran to protect it, shouting, "I understand you!"). After his death, his sister, a Nazi sympathiser, took control of his works, often editing them to fit in with her fascist viewpoint. Nietzsche's writings came to be wrongly associated with Nazism due to this editing.

Nietzsche wrote powerfully about Christianity, denouncing it as a "slave morality" that encouraged passivity in the face of injustice: rather than trying to change things, Christians were being forced to accept the status quo and disassociate from their own envy. Envy, he wrote, was a potent guide that showed us what we really wanted, and could become. The person who was able to confront their true desires and fight to realise them could become an *Übermensch*, or superman.

# EMMA GOLDMAN

## 27 JUNE 1869 – 14 MAY 1940

" If voting changed anything,
they'd make it illegal. "

EMMA GOLDMAN was an anarchist writer and activist who had a powerful influence on the development of anarchist philosophy – which argues that all government should be abolished, and society should be organised around voluntary cooperation.

Born in Russia, she fled an arranged marriage at the age of 16 and travelled to the United States to pursue her own freedom. Goldman was deeply horrified by an event in 1866, known as the Haymarket Affair, where eight workers on strike in Chicago were wrongly accused of throwing a bomb at a labour demonstration, leading to four of the workers being executed. This triggered her lifelong commitment to anarchism. She began making speeches, and found she had a mesmerising ability to inspire those who heard her. In May 1901, President William McKinley was shot and killed by Leon Czolgosz, who had heard Goldman lecture; he said he had been "set on fire" by Goldman's words.

Goldman elaborated on her ideas in her book of 1910, *Anarchism and Other Essays*. Anarchism is a political movement which was created around the belief that the state – government, big business, religious bodies – oppresses people, and therefore should be abolished. The idea was to have a society where an individual's choice to contribute replaced state enforcement of law and working conditions. With anarchism there would be rules, but no rulers.

Goldman believed passionately in her cause and spent her life travelling and lecturing on anarchism. She was imprisoned several times for her ideas, and spent time in Russia observing first-hand the dashed hopes and violence of the Russian Revolution.

# AYN RAND

## 2 FEBRUARY, 1905 – 6 MARCH, 1982

" The question isn't who is going to let me;
it's who is going to stop me. "

Born in St Petersburg in Russia, AYN RAND studied history and philosophy at the University of Petrograd, and moved to the United States in 1927, when she was 21, to become a Hollywood screenwriter. Through political activism, and later writing bestselling novels – *The Fountainhead* and *Atlas Shrugged* – and collections of essays, she went on to develop a philosophical system she called objectivism.

Objectivism holds certain things to be true: that reality exists outside of our consciousness, that our senses allow us direct contact with reality, and that reason is the only way to acquire knowledge.

Rand also claimed that the true purpose of our lives was the pursuit of our own happiness: it isn't our moral obligation to take care of anyone else. Objectivism argues that to be selfish is a rational thing to do, and that individual rights are more important than collective rights. This focus on the individual made Rand a huge influence on American conservatives and libertarians (Libertarianism is a movement which supports freedom from the state).

Rand's reaction to Communist life in Russia was at the root of her philosophy of the self. In her novel *We the Living*, she wrote, "When ... I first heard the Communist principle that Man must exist for the sake of the State, I perceived ... that this principle was evil, and that it could lead to nothing but evil." However Rand's many detractors claim that a society built on self-interest is one where greed and inequality can flourish and the most vulnerable are left unprotected.

# HANNAH ARENDT

14 OCTOBER, 1906 – 4 DECEMBER, 1975

"The sad truth is that most evil is done by people who never make up their minds to be good or evil."

HANNAH ARENDT was a Jewish philosopher and political theorist who was born in Germany, and later lived in the United States. Her work was widely admired but caused much controversy. She wrote about totalitarianism, a system of government in which the state has total control over society – notably in *Origins of Totalitarianism* (1951). But it is her writing on the trial of the Nazi war criminal Adolf Eichmann in 1963 which attracted widespread consternation and fierce criticism.

She was attacked for her idea that Eichmann (who was involved in organising the mass deportation of Jews to concentration camps) was following orders in a self-serving way rather than embodying evil. In her writing, she described his actions as an example of the "banality of evil" – how evil actions can become ordinary and everyday. This led to her being accused of lacking sympathy for the victims of the Holocaust. She received death threats and her writings are still the subject of heated debate.

During the Nazi reign, Arendt was briefly imprisoned by the Gestapo and was held in an internment camp in the south of France. She also worked with an organisation which saved thousands of children from the Holocaust.

She outraged people with her attempt to deconstruct the horrific violence of Nazism. However, she concluded her book *Eichmann in Jerusalem* by saying that she agreed that he should hang for his part in the murder of millions of people.

# SIMONE DE BEAUVOIR

9 JANUARY, 1908 – 14 APRIL, 1986

> One is not born,
> but rather becomes, a woman.

DE BEAUVOIR was a celebrated intellectual: a writer, feminist, philosopher, political activist and social theorist.

Born in Paris, France, into an educated family, she was an extremely bright child; her father would exclaim, "She thinks like a man!" It was this kind of gender stereotyping which she would later deconstruct.

She studied mathematics and then philosophy at the Sorbonne, completing her degree in 1928. As a student she distinguished herself within a group of young philosophers who became known as Existentialists (they believed that, since existence was meaningless, each individual was free to determine their own values and actions). They gave her the nickname 'the Beaver', since she worked with such commitment and focus.

Her most famous work, published in 1949, was *The Second Sex*. In this hugely influential book she gave voice to the fact that women had been oppressed for centuries by destructive ideas which cast the female as 'other' to the supposed norm of humanity: the male. This passive and secondary role limited women's choices and distorted their identities.

Her work has had a lasting and significant effect on the continuing fight for equality for women worldwide.

# FRANTZ FANON

20 JULY, 1925 – 6 DECEMBER, 1961

" What matters is not to know the
world but to change it. "

An Afro-Caribbean philosopher, psychiatrist, writer and decorated war hero, FANON was born in French-colonised Martinique. He was raised within a system that treated colonial subjects as inferior, and he spent his short life analysing, writing about, and fighting against colonisation and racism.

At the age of 18 Fanon left Martinique to fight against the Nazis in the Second World War (1939–1945); he was wounded and received the Croix de Guerre medal for his courage. However, during the war he experienced widespread racism from his white peers. He returned to Martinique in 1945 to complete his studies, then went to France to study psychiatry and medicine. During this period he wrote and published his first book *Black Faces, White Masks* which explores the negative psychological effects that colonisation and racism have upon black people.

Later, he moved to the North African country Algeria, which was under French colonial rule. He became a spokesperson for the Algerian National Liberation Front, who were trying to overthrow the government and declare Algeria independent. The French government responded to this bid for freedom with great brutality. Fanon's engagement in this conflict inspired his hugely influential book, *The Wretched of the Earth*, which defends the right of colonised people to use revolutionary violence in order to gain freedom.

Fanon died at just 36, but the influence of his work continues to be far-reaching, inspiring radical political movements all over the world.

# LUCE IRIGARAY

## 3 MAY, 1930 –

" Every desire has a relation to madness. "

LUCE IRIGARAY is a Belgian philosopher, linguist, feminist and psychoanalyst. After studying and teaching in Belgium, she moved to Paris to study philosophy and linguistics (the study of language and its structure). During this period, she also trained and worked as a psychoanalyst. It was this unique combination of interests and knowledge which led to her famous works, *Speculum of the Other Woman* (1974) and *This Sex Which is Not One* (1977). Her work focuses on how language is misused in relation to women, and how women are often referred to and treated as commodities, rather than as individuals.

In *Speculum of the Other Woman* Irigaray analysed the history of Western philosophy and psychology, just as a psychoanalyst might analyse a client. In this way she sought to draw out the unconscious of these histories and pay attention to what wasn't included, as well as what was there. In the process she identified that the universal subject (the conscious self) which is documented within Western culture was not in fact universal and neutral, but masculine, and that a suppression and denial of the feminine had taken place. She described this as 'phallocentric' – valuing and serving only men.

So controversial was this idea that the publication of this work led to Irigaray being fired from her teaching roles in two prominent French establishments. Undaunted, she continued with her work, describing and developing an ideal where culture would do justice to both sexes.

# ADRIAN PIPER

20 SEPTEMBER, 1948 –

> " I am black.
> What are you going to do about it? "

PIPER is an American artist and philosopher who lives in Berlin, Germany. She studied art and philosophy, and in 1987 she became the first ever African American woman to be granted academic tenure as a philosophy professor.

Her work in both fields discusses notions of otherness, exclusion and racism. In 'Ideology, Confrontation and Political Self-Awareness', an essay written in 1981, she examines how people hold on to certain beliefs in order to reinforce how we think of or define ourselves. Her theory is that over time these beliefs get tested but the ones that we do not challenge are those most likely to lead us to oppress others. Piper concludes her essay by telling the reader that if her piece has made them doubt their own beliefs even slightly, she will consider it a "roaring success".

As a conceptual artist, Piper has used painting, performance, installation, collage, photo-documentation and soundwork to explore her ideas. As a light-skinned black woman, one performance series saw her hand out 'calling cards' to those who had made racist comments without realising her heritage. And in her confrontational series of performances, 'The Mythic Being' (1972 – 81) she dressed as a black man and walked through crowded New York streets, asking passers-by to categorise her by race, gender and class.

Piper has said that one of her objectives for her work is to help people confront their own racist views.

# DJAMILA RIBEIRO

1 AUGUST, 1980 –

" Having the right to a voice
is having the right to humanity. "

DJAMILA RIBEIRO is a Brazilian philosopher, academic, feminist and activist. She graduated in philosophy at the Federal University of São Paulo in 2015 and continues her research there. She was also appointed deputy secretary of human rights for the city of São Paulo in 2016.

As a black feminist, Ribeiro highlights the importance of recognising intersectionality. Intersectionality is a theory which recognises that individuals can be affected by more than one form of discrimination, depending on their position within overlapping categories such as race, class, sexuality and gender, and which are usually applied to them, rather than chosen. Therefore, as Ribiero argues, a black woman might suffer from both sexism and racism, and so a 'universal' feminism cannot represent all women.

A prolific speaker and writer, she is also an online journalist and a blogger; she believes it is important for black women to use the Internet as a tool to break down the racism of the "hegemonic media" (hegemony means dominance of one state or social group over others).

Ribeiro calls for awareness of intersectionality to guide government and social policy to account for diversity – saying voices that are silenced must be heard. To listen to, and incorporate, the voices of suppressed people would mean a more creative, more humane society. She encourages everyone to strive for a fairer world, suggesting that you don't need to suffer from a form of discrimination to fight against it.

# Glossary

**ANARCHISM** – a political philosophy which believes in voluntary cooperation rather than state enforcement of law

**CLASSICISM** – the tradition of ancient Greek or Roman qualities within art and literature

**COLONISATION** – for people from one country or state to arrive in a new place and force control on the area and the people who live there

**CONSCIOUSNESS** – a state of awareness; a brain state which allows perception

**CONTROVERSIAL** – something which causes a lot of heated discussion and disagreement

**CONVENTIONAL** – to be in line with generally accepted ideas about what is usual and acceptable

**DEMOCRACY** – a system where the greatest number of votes cast by its members in an election determines who governs it

**DIALECTIC** – an exchange between people with two opposing views, in the interest of discovering the truth through reasoned argument

**DISCOURSE** – the written or spoken communication of ideas from specific societal contexts

**ENLIGHTENMENT** – an intellectual movement in late 17th and 18th century Europe which focused on reason over tradition

**ETHICS** – a personal sense of what is right and wrong, which determines how an individual behaves; also, the branch of knowledge which deals with these moral principles

**EXISTENTIALISM** – a philosophical approach concerned with the experience of human existence, where individual freedom is all and traditions of conventional morality are discarded

**GADFLY** – a fly, such as a horsefly, which bites animals; also used to describe someone who bothers others in order to provoke further thought or action

**GENDER** – a socially constructed set of ideas about women and men; different to sex, which is the biological characteristics of women and men

**GESTAPO** – the secret police in Nazi Germany from 1933 – 1945. Responsible for the murder and incarceration of those who were considered a threat to the Nazis

**HEGEMONY** – political or cultural dominance over others

**HEMLOCK** – a highly toxic, poisonous plant

**HOLOCAUST** – the genocide during the Second World War where six million Jews were murdered by Nazis. The word can also be used to refer to other incidences of mass slaughter, such as 'a nuclear holocaust'

**HUMANITY** – human beings collectively; the human race.

Also the quality of being humane: kindness and benevolence

**IDEALISM** – to have, and pursue, high principles and goals

**IMPIETY** – the lack of religious reverence

**INTERSECTIONALITY** – a theory which highlights the fact that an individual has a specific experience of oppression due to the overlap of their societal identities, in terms of race, sex, sexuality and class

**LIBERTARIANISM** – a political philosophy which upholds personal freedom as primary, and opposes state intervention

**LINGUISTICS** – the scientific study of language, including syntax, grammar and phonetics

**METAPHYSICS** – a philosophical branch which is concerned with abstract concepts such as being, identity, knowing and time

**MORALITY** – personal or societal principles related to the judgment of what is right and wrong

**NAZISM** – ideas and practices associated with the German Nazi Party which was active between 1920 – 1945; racist or authoritarian views or actions

**NEOPLATONISM** – a branch of philosophy inspired by the works of Plato, begun by Plotinus in the 3rd century CE. It considers all of existence to be derived from 'The One', a single principle

**NIHILISM** – a philosophy in which life is deemed to be completely without meaning, value or purpose; belief in nothing

**PHALLOCENTRIC** – focused on or in support of male dominance

**PROFOUND** – intense, impactful, meaningful

**PSYCHOLOGY** – the scientific study of the mind and how its functions affect behaviour

**RATIONALISM** – the philosophy that reality has a logic which can be understood through reason alone, rather than through experience; also, to base ideas and behaviour on reason rather than on emotion or religious doctrine

**ROMANTICISM** – a philosophical, artistic and literary movement of the late 18th century which valued the imagination, inspiration and nature

**SOLITUDE** – the state of being alone

**SUBJECTIVITY** – internal reality; judgement formed through personal feelings and thoughts, rather than external influences

**TOTALITARIANISM** – a system of government which demands absolute control over all aspects of individual life

**TYRANNY** – cruel abuse of power by an oppressive government or ruler

**UNCONSCIOUS** – the part of the mind that is not directly knowable to an individual, or within their control, and contains ideas and emotions which influence their thoughts and behaviour

**VIRTUE** – to have excellent moral standards, and to act like it

# Index